FAITH

FAITH

Biblical TRUTHS

— that —

Give You Wings

B&H
PUBLISHING GROUP

NASHVILLE, TENNESSEE

Published by B&H Publishing Group
Nashville, Tennessee

Dewey Decimal Classification: 242.5
Subject Heading: DEVOTIONAL LITERATURE \
BIBLE—INSPIRATION \ MEDITATIONS \ PRAYERS

1 2 3 4 5 6 7 8 • 22 21 20 19 18

CONTENTS

CONTENTS

Faith encompasses many things in this life. It is more than just a belief in something. After all, we all have believed in different things that turned out to be false. Faith is the practice and art of knowing something. Faith is almost unquestionable. We have faith that the ones we love will love us back. We have faith that our keys will unlock the doors to our homes. We have faith that the ocean will only come so far.

There are so many things in this world that we place our faith in; it's because we know that whatever will happen is expected. This does not mean that we always put our faith in the right things. You can tell this from the moments of devastation that come from something not going according to plan. The team we have faith in can lose and it will destroy us, or the childhood figure not turning out to be real breaks the child's heart when they realize it.

Our faith, our knowledge, is something that should be placed in God. We know that. Why wouldn't we place our faith in the Creator that always was, always is, and always will be?

Assurance of faith is an interesting term when we get right down to it. Assurance of something is to be confident of something, and faith is confidence in God. To put it simply, assurance of faith produces an assurance in our confidence in God. Faith is a choice. Most would agree with that, but what produces the confidence to make that choice day in and day out? God provides us with the moments in life, the trials in life, to test that faith, which inevitably produces assurance.

"Truly I tell you, anyone who hears my word and believes him who sent me has eternal life and will not come under judgment but has passed from death to life."

John 5:24

———

You did not receive a spirit of slavery to fall back into fear. Instead, you received the Spirit of adoption, by whom we cry out, "Abba, Father!" The Spirit himself testifies together with our spirit that we are God's children, and if children, also heirs— heirs of God and coheirs with Christ—if indeed we suffer with him so that we may also be glorified with him.

Romans 8:15–17

*If you confess with your mouth, "Jesus is Lord,"
and believe in your heart that God raised him from
the dead, you will be saved. One believes with the
heart, resulting in righteousness, and one confesses
with the mouth, resulting in salvation.*

    Romans 10:9–10

———

*And since we have a great high priest over the house
of God, let us draw near with a true heart in full
assurance of faith, with our hearts sprinkled clean
from an evil conscience and our bodies washed in
pure water. Let us hold on to the confession of our
hope without wavering, since he who promised is
faithful.*

    Hebrews 10:21–23

Lord God, I know that there are so many moments in my life that I look at as good or bad. Lord, give me the perspective to realize that there is more to these situations than just whether or not I like them. Put in me a spirit that seeks You more in those moments. Allow me to choose You every day so that my faith may grow. Amen

We put faith in various things in this world. Something that helps us with that faith is one's authority. For instance, you have faith when a cardiologist tells you that your heart is healthy because you trust his authority. You wouldn't necessarily have faith in his words on whether or not you need to replace a part on your car. Faith is an easy commodity when we trust the authority in front of us. God, having authority over everything, should easily gain faith from us.

Then he said to them, "Give, then, to Caesar the things that are Caesar's, and to God the things that are God's." When they heard this, they were amazed. So they left him and went away.

    Matthew 22:21–22

―――――

Jesus came near and said to them, "All authority has been given to me in heaven and on earth."

    Matthew 28:18

―――――

Let everyone submit to the governing authorities, since there is no authority except from God, and the authorities that exist are instituted by God.

    Romans 13:1

For this reason God highly exalted him and gave him the name that is above every name, so that at the name of Jesus every knee will bow—in heaven and on earth and under the earth—and every tongue will confess that Jesus Christ is Lord, to the glory of God the Father.

Philippians 2:9–11

———

Submit to every human authority because of the Lord, whether to the emperor as the supreme authority or to governors as those sent out by him to punish those who do what is evil and to praise those who do what is good. For it is God's will that you silence the ignorance of foolish people by doing good.

1 Peter 2:13–15

Heavenly Father, I know that You are good and that You are almighty. Father, allow me to trust in Your authority. Allow me see that authority more and more and recognize that it is You that is Lord over all. Lord, give me the ability to use this authority to grow deeper in faith with You. Amen

One of the most beautiful things a person can see is a sunrise. It doesn't matter where you are; there's something captivating about seeing light fill the dark world. The fact is, however, that a sunrise is so much more than just beautiful. It is an unspoken faith. A person knows each and every day that the sun will rise. They do not question it. When we realize that God is bigger than the sun, our faith can become as constant as a sunrise if we allow it.

11

*I have asked one thing from the L*ORD*;*
it is what I desire:
*to dwell in the house of the L*ORD
all the days of my life,
*gazing on the beauty of the L*ORD
and seeking him in his temple.
   Psalm 27:4

———

I will praise you
because I have been remarkably and wondrously
made.
Your works are wondrous,
and I know this very well.
   Psalm 139:14

Charm is deceptive and beauty is fleeting,
but a woman who fears the LORD will be praised.
  Proverbs 31:30

———

You are absolutely beautiful, my darling;
there is no imperfection in you.
  Song of Songs 4:7

———

Don't let your beauty consist of outward things like
elaborate hairstyles and wearing gold jewelry, but
rather what is inside the heart—the imperishable
quality of a gentle and quiet spirit, which is of great
worth in God's sight.
  1 Peter 3:3–4

Lord God, thank You for all of the amazing things that You have created. Thank You for the awe-inspiring beauty that I get to see every day. Lord, I know that there are so many beautiful things that You've created to instill a faith in You. Lord, continue creating these things, so that I can be reminded each day of how amazing You are. Amen

When we have faith in God, there are a great deal of blessings that come from following after Him. One of those is recognizing blessings as they come. When a woman was spending her last moments on earth, she said that it was such a blessing. Her family looked at each other, puzzled over her words. Her response to their puzzled looks was, "You all still come together as a family, regardless of distance, when family needs you." Blessings are found easily when your faith is strong. It's shown in recognizing where God is in the tough moments.

"May the LORD bless you and protect you; may the LORD make his face shine on you and be gracious to you; may the LORD look with favor on you and give you peace."

Numbers 6:24–26

———

Indeed, we have all received grace upon grace from his fullness, for the law was given through Moses; grace and truth came through Jesus Christ.

John 1:16–17

———

And God is able to make every grace overflow to you, so that in every way, always having everything you need, you may excel in every good work.

2 Corinthians 9:8

Blessed is the God and Father of our Lord Jesus Christ, who has blessed us with every spiritual blessing in the heavens in Christ.

 Ephesians 1:3

———

And my God will supply all your needs according to his riches in glory in Christ Jesus.

 Philippians 4:19

Father, I know that there are so many moments that come into my life that I don't recognize as blessings. Lord, I'm sorry that so many of Your blessings have passed by and I don't even acknowledge them. Allow me to be more aware of the blessings that You give daily, that I might grow a deeper faith in You. Amen

It's hard to think about a bold faith and not think of the young David. As a teenager, he took on Goliath and defeated him with one stone. It wasn't even really a battle. David was known specifically not so much for his defeat of the giant as much as he was known for his boldness in faith before he took on Goliath. He knew he was going to win because of his faith in God.

*The wicked flee when no one is pursuing them,
but the righteous are as bold as a lion.*
    Proverbs 28:1

———

*Since, then, we have such a hope, we act with great
boldness.*
    2 Corinthians 3:12

———

*In him we have boldness and confident access
through faith in him.*
    Ephesians 3:12

For God has not given us a spirit of fear, but one of power, love, and sound judgment.

2 Timothy 1:7

———

Therefore, let us approach the throne of grace with boldness, so that we may receive mercy and find grace to help us in time of need.

Hebrews 4:16

God, I know that You are a mighty God. I know that You have created all things and are over all things. Lord, even though I know these things . . . I don't act like it. I've shared my faith in whispers, if I even do that. Lord, put in me a bold spirit that professes You. Give me a boldness that the world can see, and allow them to see that this boldness comes from You. Amen

Every morning for sixty years, Edgar's wife made him breakfast. She made him the same thing every day: two eggs, two pieces of bacon, and two pieces of toast. Even when the two went on vacation, she found a way to get him that breakfast. One morning, however, she didn't make breakfast. She fell ill, and for the next three months, he cared for her. Saddened and frustrated by the situation, Edgar held his wife's hand and said, "I always had faith that you'd make me breakfast." Her response? "Edgar, you had faith in my love, not those eggs. I've gotten up every morning and had that for you." We have a God that cares for us everyday. His care is something in which we should have faith.

*"I give you a new command: Love one another.
Just as I have loved you, you are also to love one
another. By this everyone will know that you are my
disciples, if you love one another."*
    John 13:34–35

———

*Carry one another's burdens; in this way you will
fulfill the law of Christ.*
    Galatians 6:2

Therefore, as we have opportunity, let us work for the good of all, especially for those who belong to the household of faith.

Galatians 6:10

———

Everyone should look out not only for his own interests, but also for the interests of others.

Philippians 2:4

Heavenly Father, I know that You care for me. I know that You provide for my needs. Lord, I admit that sometimes I come to expect that care without thanking You. Thank You, Father, for loving me and caring for me. Allow me to take as much care of my family as You take care of me. Amen

Most children have an interesting sense of faith. Some expect to always find a present under the tree at Christmas. Some expect to never get seriously injured. Some know that they will always have a certain friend. Faith is not so much belief with them as much as it is a knowing. There's a reason we are called children of God. We cannot simply believe that God loves us. We must take on the faith of a child and know it.

"Blessed are the peacemakers, for they will be called sons of God."

Matthew 5:9

———

But to all who did receive him, he gave them the right to be children of God, to those who believe in his name, who were born, not of natural descent, or of the will of the flesh, or of the will of man, but of God.

John 1:12–13

———

For through faith you are all sons of God in Christ Jesus.

Galatians 3:26

The Spirit himself testifies together with our spirit that we are God's children, and if children, also heirs—heirs of God and coheirs with Christ—if indeed we suffer with him so that we may also be glorified with him.

   Romans 8:16–17

―――

See what great love the Father has given us that we should be called God's children—and we are! The reason the world does not know us is that it didn't know him.

   1 John 3:1

Father, I know there are so many moments where I have to believe that You love me. I have to say it out loud to remind myself of my beliefs. Father, move me away from believing and move me into knowing. Allow me to know You love me each and every day. Give me the ability to see with knowledge and confidence that You love me on a level I'll never understand. Amen

There was an atheist in an office building. He wasn't the only one, but he was probably the most vocal about his atheism. His life, however, was changed when an old custodian got on an elevator with him. The custodian looked at the man, said nothing, then reached in his jacket and gave him a pocket Bible. When the atheist told the old man he wasn't a believer, the old man looked at him as he got off the elevator and said "I have faith that there is a heaven and a hell . . . how much do I have to hate you to not try and tell you about it?" The atheist says it was the most compassionate thing he'd ever heard from a Christian. If we have faith, we have to be willing to take steps of compassion toward others, no matter their faith, or lack of.

Yet he was compassionate;
he atoned for their iniquity
and did not destroy them.
He often turned his anger aside
and did not unleash all his wrath.
   Psalm 78:38

———

When he went ashore, he saw a large crowd and
had compassion on them, because they were like
sheep without a shepherd. Then he began to teach
them many things.
   Mark 6:34

Carry one another's burdens; in this way you will fulfill the law of Christ.
    Galatians 6:2

———

And be kind and compassionate to one another, forgiving one another, just as God also forgave you in Christ.
    Ephesians 4:32

Lord Jesus, I have not acted compassionately toward others. I know that I have faith in You, but I don't share that faith. Lord, I know that this is not loving. Instill in me a heart for people so that I may share Your message with others, so that they may know You. Amen

Confidence is something that comes with preparation. Confident teachers have prepared lessons. Confident athletes have prepared through training and practice. Confident musicians have skill that has been prepared throughout the years. A confident student walks into an exam prepared through studying. Was this preparation easy? Of course not, but through hardship confidence is developed. Faith is the same way. Through hardship, our confidence is sharpened by our faith in God.

Do not fear, for I am with you; do not be afraid, for I am your God. I will strengthen you; I will help you; I will hold on to you with my righteous right hand.
   Isaiah 41:10

———

It is not that we are competent in ourselves to claim anything as coming from ourselves, but our adequacy is from God.
   2 Corinthians 3:5

———

I am able to do all things through him who strengthens me.
   Philippians 4:13

So don't throw away your confidence, which has a great reward. For you need endurance, so that after you have done God's will, you may receive what was promised.

Hebrews 10:35–36

———

This is how we will know that we belong to the truth and will reassure our hearts before him whenever our hearts condemn us; for God is greater than our hearts, and he knows all things. Dear friends, if our hearts don't condemn us, we have confidence before God and receive whatever we ask from him because we keep his commands and do what is pleasing in his sight.

1 John 3:19–22

Lord, I know that during many hardships in my life, I never said thank You. Father, I know that from those bad times, there were good things to learn; and even though I would not want to relive them, I would never trade those hard times for anything because of the good You have shown me through them. Allow me to have faith when hard times come again. Amen

There are moments in life that seem daunting. There are many trials that we go through. One thing we have to remember, however, is that having courage and having faith does not equal fearlessness. Firemen do not run into burning buildings with a fearless attitude. They have faith in their training and equipment, and that is what gives them courage. Like firemen, God equips us to go through the fires in our lives. It doesn't mean that the flames lose their danger; it simply means that we can have courage knowing that God is with us.

Haven't I commanded you: be strong and courageous? Do not be afraid or discouraged, for the LORD your God is with you wherever you go.

   Joshua 1:9

———

I always let the LORD guide me.
Because he is at my right hand,
I will not be shaken.

   Psalm 16:8

Wait for the LORD*;*
be strong, and let your heart be courageous.
Wait for the LORD*.*
    Psalm 27:14

———

Be alert, stand firm in the faith, be courageous, be
strong.
    1 Corinthians 16:13

———

For God has not given us a spirit of fear, but one of
power, love, and sound judgment.
    2 Timothy 1:7

Father, I know that You are with me. I know that there are so many moments that come into my life when I feel like You are not there, and that's wrong. Father, continue to be with me as I go through these trials. Allow me to have courage in knowing that my faith in You is what will get me through this time. Amen

In marriage, you enter into a covenant with God to stand by your spouse till death parts you. It's more than a promise. It's an oath. It's something that stands the test of time. A covenant is meant to last forever. Whenever a covenant is broken or changed, there is a price. When divorce happens, people pay for it with heartache and despair. With God's new covenant with man, that price was paid with the sacrifice of His Son. With such a price, our faith in God's love for us should be unshakable.

He remembers his covenant forever,
the promise he ordained
for a thousand generations—
the covenant he made with Abraham,
swore to Isaac,
and confirmed to Jacob as a decree
and to Israel as a permanent covenant:
"I will give the land of Canaan to you as your
inherited portion."
　　Psalm 105:8–11

———

Therefore, he is the mediator of a new covenant, so
that those who are called might receive the promise
of the eternal inheritance, because a death has
taken place for redemption from the transgressions
committed under the first covenant.
　　Hebrews 9:15

"Look, the days are coming"—this is the LORD's declaration—"when I will make a new covenant with the house of Israel and with the house of Judah. This one will not be like the covenant I made with their ancestors on the day I took them by the hand to lead them out of the land of Egypt—my covenant that they broke even though I am their master"—the LORD's declaration. "Instead, this is the covenant I will make with the house of Israel after those days"—the LORD's declaration. "I will put my teaching within them and write it on their hearts. I will be their God, and they will be my people. No longer will one teach his neighbor or his brother, saying, 'Know the LORD,' for they will all know me, from the least to the greatest of them"— this is the Lord's declaration. "For I will forgive their iniquity and never again remember their sin."

Jeremiah 31:31–34

Heavenly Father, thank You for sending Your Son down to us. I know that it was a heavy price to be paid. I know that through this we are able to get to You, Father. Allow me to continue to grow in faith with You, Lord. Be with me, Lord, and remind me daily of the price that had to be paid . . . to save me. Amen

Faith is a constant act. It is not something that we simply build up to and never have to touch again. Tending to one's faith is similar to tending a garden. You do not simply throw the seeds out into the soil. You water them, tend to them when they sprout, care for them in order to yield harvest, and then use those seeds to continue the gardening process in the coming years. It takes a certain level of devotion to tend a garden. It takes it even more to tend to one's faith.

This book of instruction must not depart from your mouth; you are to meditate on it day and night so that you may carefully observe everything written in it. For then you will prosper and succeed in whatever you do.

Joshua 1:8

———

For where your treasure is, there your heart will be also.

Luke 12:34

"No servant can serve two masters, since either he will hate one and love the other, or he will be devoted to one and despise the other. You cannot serve both God and money."

    Luke 16:13

———

Be diligent to present yourself to God as one approved, a worker who doesn't need to be ashamed, correctly teaching the word of truth.

    2 Timothy 2:15

Lord, I'm sorry. I have not tended to my relationship with You the way that I know I should. Lord, there are so many things in this world that I have let distract me from my devotion to You. Father, allow me to overcome those distractions so that I may have a deeper faith and relationship with You. Amen

Faith and discernment go hand in hand. Many of us can look back to a time when we've acted with faith without discernment, and it has cost us in the end. Some of us come upon opportunities or relationships and because we want them, we assume that God's hand is on them. How do we discern what the right thing to do is, then? Through prayer and faith, we make the best decisions we can. It doesn't mean we'll always make the right call, but our discernment weakens if we don't act with God.

So give your servant a receptive heart to judge your people and to discern between good and evil. For who is able to judge this great people of yours?

    1 Kings 3:9

———

And I pray this: that your love will keep on growing in knowledge and every kind of discernment, so that you may approve the things that are superior and may be pure and blameless in the day of Christ.

    Philippians 1:9–10

———

Don't stifle the Spirit. Don't despise prophecies, but test all things. Hold on to what is good. Stay away from every kind of evil.

    1 Thessalonians 5:19–22

*Now if any of you lacks wisdom, he should
ask God—who gives to all generously and
ungrudgingly—and it will be given to him.*
   James 1:5

———

*Dear friends, do not believe every spirit, but test the
spirits to see if they are from God, because many
false prophets have gone out into the world.*
   1 John 4:1

Father, there are so many times that I've put my want above Your wisdom. There are so many times that my discernment has been poor because I've acted without your blessing. I've made mistakes that didn't have to happen simply because I wasn't acting with You. Lord, continue to be with me. Allow me to make decisions with You and not on my own. Amen

Money is one of the things that never satisfies people. Millions of people all over the world work harder and harder to make more money, and no matter how much they make, it never seems to be enough. The problem is that these people put their faith in this idea that one day, there will be enough. One day, they'll get the right paycheck and they won't have to worry about anything else. Putting faith in the things of this world will leave you dissatisfied; only faith in God can satisfy.

For he has satisfied the thirsty
and filled the hungry with good things.
  Psalm 107:9

———

You open your hand
and satisfy the desire of every living thing.
  Psalm 145:16

———

The LORD will always lead you, satisfy you in a
parched land, and strengthen your bones. You will
be like a watered garden and like a spring whose
water never runs dry.
  Isaiah 58:11

"I am the bread of life," Jesus told them. "No one who comes to me will ever be hungry, and no one who believes in me will ever be thirsty again."

John 6:35

———

Now may the God of hope fill you with all joy and peace as you believe so that you may overflow with hope by the power of the Holy Spirit.

Romans 15:13

Heavenly Father, I know that there are so many things that I am dissatisfied with. I feel like I can't find satisfaction in anything I pursue . . . except You. I'm sorry that I have chased after the things of this world, God. Allow me to chase after You, for I know that it is only You that can satisfy. Amen

One of the most incredible parts about the early church is the story of Paul. After his revelation on the road to Damascus, he incurred many hardships. One of his most famous hardships was his time in prison. From this time, he kept his faith in God and wrote Ephesians, Philippians, Colossians, and Philemon. He felt encouraged enough, in prison, to write the very letters that would be included in the New Testament.

The Lord is the one who will go before you. He will be with you; he will not leave you or abandon you. Do not be afraid or discouraged.

Deuteronomy 31:8

———

God is our refuge and strength,
a helper who is always found
in times of trouble.

Psalm 46:1

———

"Aren't five sparrows sold for two pennies? Yet not one of them is forgotten in God's sight. Indeed, the hairs of your head are all counted. Don't be afraid; you are worth more than many sparrows."

Luke 12:6–7

"*I have told you these things so that in me you may have peace. You will have suffering in this world. Be courageous! I have conquered the world.*"
   John 16:33

———

And let us watch out for one another to provoke love and good works, not neglecting to gather together, as some are in the habit of doing, but encouraging each other, and all the more as you see the day approaching.
   Hebrews 10:24–25

Lord, I am so discouraged with the things of this world. I feel like I cannot get anything right. Lord, give me courage to take on the obstacles in this world. Thank You for being with me, Lord. Thank You for never leaving my side. Remind me of this so that I constantly may be encouraged. Amen

There's an old man that restores classic cars as a hobby. He's worked on hundreds of projects, but there's one car he's never sold: a 1967 Chevy Impala, the first car he ever owned. He works on it everyday. He finds something new to do to it every chance he gets. That car has had seven engines replaced, seventy-six tires changed, upholstery changed four times, and every five years has had a new paint job. His friends have told him that he'll make that car last forever. We know it won't actually last forever, but how many of us can say that we work on our faith with the same kind of dedication?

Before the mountains were born,
before you gave birth to the earth and the world,
from eternity to eternity, you are God.
    Psalm 90:2

———

He has made everything appropriate in its time.
He has also put eternity in their hearts, but no
one can discover the work God has done from
beginning to end.
    Ecclesiastes 3:11

———

For the wages of sin is death, but the gift of God is
eternal life in Christ Jesus our Lord.
    Romans 6:23

"Truly I tell you, anyone who hears my word and believes him who sent me has eternal life and will not come under judgment but has passed from death to life."

John 5:24

———

"This is eternal life: that they may know you, the only true God, and the one you have sent—Jesus Christ."

John 17:3

Lord God, I know that there are so many things in this world that are temporary that I treat like they will be around forever. It is because of this lie that I put You second to so many things. I'm sorry for that, Lord. Father, remind me daily that You are eternal, and that my relationship and faith with You is what should hold my focus. Amen

To be full of faith is probably one of the most honorable things to have as a believer. It means something rather simple, but is something that is so easily overlooked. To be full of faith means that no matter what may come from the world, God always is and always will be. When we have faith in the constant love of God, the world's issues seem to be overshadowed by that love.

Because of the LORD's faithful love
we do not perish,
for his mercies never end.
They are new every morning;
great is your faithfulness!
    Lamentations 3:22–23

———

If we are faithless, he remains faithful, for he
cannot deny himself.
    2 Timothy 2:13

———

Let us hold on to the confession of our hope without
wavering, since he who promised is faithful.
    Hebrews 10:23

"*His master said to him, 'Well done, good and faithful servant! You were faithful over a few things; I will put you in charge of many things. Share your master's joy.'*"
    Matthew 25:21

———

"*Whoever is faithful in very little is also faithful in much, and whoever is unrighteous in very little is also unrighteous in much. So if you have not been faithful with worldly wealth, who will trust you with what is genuine? And if you have not been faithful with what belongs to someone else, who will give you what is your own?*"
    Luke 16:10–12

Father, forgive me. I have put such a focus on this world that I've forgotten just what it means to have Your unfailing love. Lord, remind me daily what it means to have a life full of faith. Remind me that no matter what may happen in this world, You will always be there. Thank You for never failing, Lord. Amen

In schools all over the country, however, introverted students are forced to stand and present projects. Introverts will normally live in fear of these days. How do they cope? They over-prepare. They say their presentation over and over again until it is memorized. Because of this, they have faith their presentation will be a success. When we spend time with God, whether it be through the Word or prayer, we build faith with Him that allows us to take on the obstacles of the world. It's something we need to do day in and day out, over and over again, so that our faith, like a prepared introvert, is unshakable.

Haven't I commanded you: be strong and courageous? Do not be afraid or discouraged, for the LORD *your God is with you wherever you go.*

 Joshua 1:9

———

When I am afraid,
I will trust in you.
 Psalm 56:3

———

You did not receive a spirit of slavery to fall back into fear. Instead, you received the Spirit of adoption, by whom we cry out, "Abba, Father!"
 Romans 8:15

For God has not given us a spirit of fear, but one of power, love, and sound judgment.

    2 Timothy 1:7

———

Humble yourselves, therefore, under the mighty hand of God, so that he may exalt you at the proper time, casting all your cares on him, because he cares about you.

    1 Peter 5:6–7

Heavenly Father, I have allowed my faith to be shaken. I have become afraid. I know that this is not right. I know that it is only through You that I can overcome this fear. Lord, allow me to strengthen my faith in You. Place in me a heart that moves forward with courage. Thank You for being with me, Lord, and showing that with You, I have nothing to fear. Amen

One of the statements we hear often from people that are struggling with conflict is the question, "Why should I forgive them, when I know they are only going to hurt me again?" Pastors who specialize in conflict resolution can tell you that one of the most important aspects of forgiveness is faith. You don't put your faith in that person that just let you down, of course. That would be silly. You put your faith in God. God has forgiven you for your wrong, and He has forgiven the wrongdoer for theirs. If you have faith in a God that forgives, then why can't you forgive?

"Therefore I tell you, her many sins have been forgiven; that's why she loved much. But the one who is forgiven little, loves little."

Luke 7:47

———

Live in harmony with one another. Do not be proud; instead, associate with the humble. Do not be wise in your own estimation. Do not repay anyone evil for evil. Give careful thought to do what is honorable in everyone's eyes. If possible, as far as it depends on you, live at peace with everyone.

Romans 12:16–18

Be kind and compassionate to one another,
forgiving one another, just as God also forgave you
in Christ.

    Ephesians 4:32

———

As God's chosen ones, holy and dearly loved, put on
compassion, kindness, humility, gentleness, and
patience, bearing with one another and forgiving
one another if anyone has a grievance against
another. Just as the Lord has forgiven you, so you
are also to forgive.

    Colossians 3:12–13

Lord, I know that I need to fix this wedge that is keeping me from loving those around me. There are people that have hurt me, and God, I'm afraid to allow them back into my life. I feel like they are only going to hurt me again. Lord, soften my heart. Remove the things in my life that keep me from forgiving others. Thank You, Lord, for forgiving me when I have failed You. Allow me to do the same for those that have failed me. Amen

Many don't realize it, but faith is one of the most important aspects of friendship. We work on our friendships. We talk to our friends at least once or twice a week. We spend time with them when we can. We even take the time to pray for them and their family. Because of our constant working on those friendships, we have faith in the continuation of that friendship. It's easy to say things like "We'll be friends forever" when we take the time to work on that friendship. We instinctively have faith in the relationships we work on diligently. How are you working on your relationship with God?

Iron sharpens iron,
and one person sharpens another.
　　Proverbs 27:17

———

Two are better than one because they have a good
reward for their efforts. For if either falls, his
companion can lift him up; but pity the one who
falls without another to lift him up.
　　Ecclesiastes 4:9–10

———

Dear friends, let us love one another, because love is
from God, and everyone who loves has been born of
God and knows God.
　　1 John 4:7

"No one has greater love than this: to lay down his life for his friends. You are my friends if you do what I command you. I do not call you servants anymore, because a servant doesn't know what his master is doing. I have called you friends, because I have made known to you everything I have heard from my Father."

John 15:13–15

———

Therefore encourage one another and build each other up as you are already doing.

1 Thessalonians 5:11

Father, thank You for friends. Thank You for placing people in my life that help me to grow, that sharpen me. Lord, I know that there are many times that I would have fallen if not for my friends. Father, thank You for being there when they couldn't. Please continue to be with me, and allow me the opportunities to be the kind of friend that You would have me be. Amen

GRACE

When Jonathan missed the game winning catch, he walked to his coach after the game. His head was low, and he barely got out in a breaking voice that he was sorry. The coach sighed, put his hand on the boy's helmet, and said, "Son, you stay after practice to get better. You're the first to workouts, and you've led this team through a tough season. When you work like you do, I can't fault you for missing a catch." The coach showed Jonathan grace simply because he had faith in Jonathan's character. He knew who Jonathan was. God gives us grace for our mistakes everyday. The reason? It's because He knows us and loves us.

The law came along to multiply the trespass. But where sin multiplied, grace multiplied even more.
Romans 5:20

———

For sin will not rule over you, because you are not under the law but under grace.
Romans 6:14

———

Now if by grace, then it is not by works; otherwise grace ceases to be grace.
Romans 11:6

But he said to me, "My grace is sufficient for you, for my power is perfected in weakness." Therefore, I will most gladly boast all the more about my weaknesses, so that Christ's power may reside in me.

2 Corinthians 12:9

———

For you are saved by grace through faith, and this is not from yourselves; it is God's gift—not from works, so that no one can boast.

Ephesians 2:8–9

Lord, thank You for grace. I know there are so many times in my life that I fall short or fail You, and yet You still give me grace. You recognize my lack of protection and you still accept me. Thank You for loving me like that. Lord, allow me to give others grace. Allow me to recognize that I am not perfect, and because of that I have no reason to withhold grace from others. Amen

GUILT

All of us carry guilt to some degree. Some of us have seen the toll the weight of guilt can hold on a person. One of the things that we see often is the debilitating guilt carried by ex-convicts. Because of their pasts, they feel as if they are not allowed to move forward in society. They often have to be reminded that their debt has been paid. Some of us have similar feelings toward God. We allow our guilt to keep us from moving forward with Him. Remember, Christ did not choose people that were perfect; He chose those that were willing to let go of their guilt and move forward with Him.

As far as the east is from the west,
so far has he removed
our transgressions from us.
  Psalm 103:12

———

"Come, let us settle this," says the LORD. "Though
your sins are scarlet, they will be as white as snow;
though they are crimson red, they will be like wool."
  Isaiah 1:18

———

Therefore, there is now no condemnation for those
in Christ Jesus, because the law of the Spirit of life
in Christ Jesus has set you free from the law of sin
and death.
  Romans 8:1–2

In him we have redemption through his blood,
the forgiveness of our trespasses, according to the
riches of his grace.
  Ephesians 1:7

———

If we confess our sins, he is faithful and righteous
to forgive us our sins and to cleanse us from all
unrighteousness.
  1 John 1:9

Lord, I know that I am guilty of sin. I have wronged You today. For that I am guilty. Father, I know that guilt over something is going to happen; but I know that if I stay here, I won't be able to move forward with You. I know that if I allow this guilt to control me, I won't allow myself to be forgiven. Father, thank You for forgiving me of my sins. Allow me to move forward as one that is redeemed and not one that is still guilty. Amen

There's a veteran that received the news that he would never walk correctly again. He spent the next few decades accepting that until the day he decided to take action. He started exercising—trying to walk without his canes, and he fell. He fell everyday. Something he said, though, is what captured faith, "Just because I can't do it today, doesn't mean I won't do it tomorrow." Faith is something that grows, but without constant work, your faith will only get you as far as a couple of canes. The doctors were right in that he doesn't walk . . . simply because he chooses to run.

But those who trust in the L<small>ORD</small> *will renew their strength; they will soar on wings like eagles; they will run and not become weary, they will walk and not faint.*

    Isaiah 40:31

———

I wait for the L<small>ORD</small>*; I wait and put my hope in his word.*

    Psalm 130:5

———

Now may the God of hope fill you with all joy and peace as you believe so that you may overflow with hope by the power of the Holy Spirit.

    Romans 15:13

We have also obtained access through him by faith into this grace in which we stand, and we rejoice in the hope of the glory of God. And not only that, but we also rejoice in our afflictions, because we know that affliction produces endurance, endurance produces proven character, and proven character produces hope.

Romans 5:2–4

———

Let us run with endurance the race that lies before us, keeping our eyes on Jesus, the source and perfecter of our faith. For the joy that lay before him, he endured the cross, despising the shame, and sat down at the right hand of the throne of God. For consider him who endured such hostility from sinners against himself, so that you won't grow weary and give up.

Hebrews 12:1–3

Lord Jesus, thank You for providing the ultimate hope of man. Thank You for dying on the cross so that I may be able to live forever with You. Lord, there are so many moments in this life that need hope. Please allow for those moments as we go throughout our days here. Lord, instill in me a spirit that drives to share that hope with others. Amen

There's humility in losing a job. When Reese lost her job, her father asked her, "Were you acting like an employee or one who lost their job?" When she asked what the difference was, he told her that employees act out a faith in the company while at work, and those who lose their job act out a faith that's outside of the company while at work. Reese's eyes went down to the ground. She realized which one she had been. In faith, there's an attitude attached to it. We can't expect to have a strong faith in anything if we are not working with that faith everyday.

Sitting down, he called the Twelve and said to them, "If anyone wants to be first, he must be last and servant of all."

Mark 9:35

———

Live in harmony with one another. Do not be proud; instead, associate with the humble. Do not be wise in your own estimation.

Romans 12:16

———

Do nothing out of selfish ambition or conceit, but in humility consider others as more important than yourselves.

Philippians 2:3

Adopt the same attitude as that of Christ Jesus, who, existing in the form of God, did not consider equality with God as something to be exploited. Instead he emptied himself by assuming the form of a servant, taking on the likeness of humanity. And when he had come as a man, he humbled himself by becoming obedient to the point of death—even to death on a cross.

    Philippians 2:5–8

———

Who among you is wise and understanding? By his good conduct he should show that his works are done in the gentleness that comes from wisdom.

    James 3:13

Lord, I know that there are moments that I have had to be humbled. Lord, thank You for humbling me during the moments that I needed it the most. Father, place in me a heart of humility. Allow me to look at the dark moments in life as a way to grow . . . as a way to learn. Amen

A man had two sons. One of the brothers finally looked to the father and asked the question most parents have gotten at least once. "Why does he get to drive your car, and I don't?" He had to deliver one of the many tough talks that comes with parenting. He said, "Well, son, your brother has earned my trust with the car because I've seen how he drives. He doesn't go over the speed limit, he keeps his eyes on the road, and he goes where he says he goes and nowhere else." The brother did not push any further because he knew his integrity as a driver was not as exemplary. Having faith in those with integrity is natural. The integrity of God is never failing. Look to Him in faith.

The one who lives with integrity lives securely,
but whoever perverts his ways will be found out.
    Proverbs 10:9

———

Better the poor person who lives with integrity
than the rich one who distorts right and wrong.
    Proverbs 28:6

———

Indeed, we are giving careful thought to do what
is right, not only before the Lord but also before
people.
    2 Corinthians 8:21

Whatever you do, do it from the heart, as something done for the Lord and not for people, knowing that you will receive the reward of an inheritance from the Lord. You serve the Lord Christ.
   Colossians 3:23–24

———

Yet do this with gentleness and respect, keeping a clear conscience, so that when you are accused, those who disparage your good conduct in Christ will be put to shame.
   1 Peter 3:16

Lord, I know that I need to work on my integrity. I have acted selfishly. Lord, put in me a heart that desires to do the right thing. Give me the discernment to know what is right and put in me a spirit to chase after what is right. Father, You know my heart, allow me to overcome my selfishness and act in a way that is pleasing to You. Amen

One's knowledge can lead to many things. Several jobs are completely dependent upon one's knowledge. How does one gain this knowledge? Well, a person has to take the time to develop that knowledge. It takes time, study, and dedication. Most people aren't willing to build their own knowledge because of the work attached to it. We build our knowledge in who God is through constantly working on our relationship with Him. We pray, study, and contemplate on what His will is for us. It takes a lot of work, but strong faith is like knowledge. It holds a value that few can comprehend.

For wisdom will enter your heart,
and knowledge will delight you.
    Proverbs 2:10

———

The mind of the discerning acquires knowledge,
and the ear of the wise seeks it.
    Proverbs 18:15

———

We know that "we all have knowledge." Knowledge
puffs up, but love builds up. If anyone thinks he
knows anything, he does not yet know it as he
ought to know it. But if anyone loves God, he is
known by him.
    1 Corinthians 8:1–3

For the earth will be filled with the knowledge of the LORD's glory, as the water covers the sea.

    Habakkuk 2:14

———

For this reason also, since the day we heard this, we haven't stopped praying for you. We are asking that you may be filled with the knowledge of his will in all wisdom and spiritual understanding, so that you may walk worthy of the Lord, fully pleasing to him: bearing fruit in every good work and growing in the knowledge of God, being strengthened with all power, according to his glorious might, so that you may have great endurance and patience, joyfully giving thanks to the Father, who has enabled you to share in the saints' inheritance in the light.

    Colossians 1:9–12

Father, I have come to know amazing things about You. Through studying Your Word and listening to the wisdom of those that follow after You daily, I have come to know You on a level I never thought I could. Lord, I know there is so much more that I just don't know. Place in me a heart that continues to want to know more about You each day. Amen

A man pulled his new son-in-law to the side at the reception. He looked at him with tear filled eyes and said, "I have wiped that girl's tears. I have protected her since the day she was born. I have loved her and prayed for her since before she was born, and I prayed for you before I knew you. I had faith that God would provide my daughter a man that could do for her what I have and more. I have faith in you, son, because I've seen the way you love her, and how it is a constant devotion that doesn't stop working." Like love, we don't simply reach a spot in our faith where we're done working on it. Work on your faith everyday, the same way you work on love everyday.

"But I say to you who listen: Love your enemies, do what is good to those who hate you, bless those who curse you, pray for those who mistreat you."
    Luke 6:27–28

———

Love is patient, love is kind. Love does not envy, is not boastful, is not arrogant, is not rude, is not self-seeking, is not irritable, and does not keep a record of wrongs.
    1 Corinthians 13:4–5

———

Above all, maintain constant love for one another, since love covers a multitude of sins.
    1 Peter 4:8

God's love was revealed among us in this way: God sent his one and only Son into the world so that we might live through him.

1 John 4:9

———

And we have come to know and to believe the love that God has for us. God is love, and the one who remains in love remains in God, and God remains in him.

1 John 4:16

Heavenly Father, thank You for love. Thank You for the people that I love, and thank You for the people that love me. Lord, I know that love is something that I constantly have to work on. Put in me a spirit that works on that love daily. Allow me to love others, God, as You have loved me. Amen

Some people struggle with mercy. They think that there are so many things that they've done that would keep God from showing them mercy. Some have pointed to a sin they deemed unforgivable. We, however, can have faith in His mercy. He gave His Son for us, after all. Making such a sacrifice was the greatest act of mercy that could ever be. This act was done to pay for the debt of ALL sin. Know that God has shown you mercy. Have faith in Him and the mercy He has shown you.

"Blessed are the merciful, for they will be shown mercy."

Matthew 5:7

———

"Go and learn what this means: I desire mercy and not sacrifice. For I didn't come to call the righteous, but sinners."

Matthew 9:13

———

Therefore, let us approach the throne of grace with boldness, so that we may receive mercy and find grace to help us in time of need.

Hebrews 4:16

Speak and act as those who are to be judged by the law of freedom. For judgment is without mercy to the one who has not shown mercy. Mercy triumphs over judgment.

James 2:12–13

———

Blessed be the God and Father of our Lord Jesus Christ. Because of his great mercy he has given us new birth into a living hope through the resurrection of Jesus Christ from the dead.

1 Peter 1:3

Lord Jesus, thank You for dying on the cross for my sins. Thank You for showing the greatest act of mercy that's ever been. Lord, right now, there are those in this world that need more mercy from me. Allow me to show others mercy as You have shown me each day. Amen

When one has a strong faith, praise turns into a desire. We have faith in the God that sent His Son to die for us so that we may have eternal life. We have faith in the God that knew that man could not do it on his own, and it was because of this knowledge that He sent His Son to pay the ultimate price for us. When we have faith in the God that did that for us, it only seems natural to praise Him.

I will praise God's name with song
and exalt him with thanksgiving.
 Psalm 69:30

———

Hallelujah!
Praise God in his sanctuary.
Praise him in his mighty expanse.
Praise him for his powerful acts;
praise him for his abundant greatness.
 Psalm 150:1–2

*For from him and through him and to him are all
things. To him be the glory forever. Amen.*

Romans 11:36

———

*Now to him who is able to protect you from
stumbling and to make you stand in the presence of
his glory, without blemish and with great joy, to the
only God our Savior, through Jesus Christ our Lord,
be glory, majesty, power, and authority before all
time, now and forever. Amen.*

Jude 24–25

Heavenly Father, thank You. Thank You for giving me the talents and gifts that I have. Thank You for giving me the love that I don't deserve each day. Thank You for loving me, for forgiving me, for looking down on me with grace and mercy. Instill in me a heart that recognizes Your love each day, and remind me to praise You every day that You love me. Amen

Prayer is one of the most important parts of acting out one's faith. Yes, we pray over meals and before we go to bed, and even to start and end our day, but prayer is something that is simply taking action to reach out and connect with God. This action is one of the building blocks to one's faith. You cannot build faith without prayer. Constantly reach out to God so that your faith may grow.

"Whenever you pray, you must not be like the hypocrites, because they love to pray standing in the synagogues and on the street corners to be seen by people. . . . But when you pray, go into your private room, shut your door, and pray to your Father who is in secret. And your Father who sees in secret will reward you. When you pray, don't babble like the Gentiles, since they imagine they'll be heard for their many words. Don't be like them, because your Father knows the things you need before you ask him.

"Therefore, you should pray like this: Our Father in heaven, your name be honored as holy. Your kingdom come. Your will be done on earth as it is in heaven. Give us today our daily bread. And forgive us our debts, as we also have forgiven our debtors. . . .

"For if you forgive others their offenses, your heavenly Father will forgive you as well. But if you don't forgive others, your Father will not forgive your offenses."

Matthew 6:5–14

In the same way the Spirit also helps us in our weakness, because we do not know what to pray for as we should, but the Spirit himself intercedes for us with unspoken groanings.

Romans 8:26

———

Don't worry about anything, but in everything, through prayer and petition with thanksgiving, present your requests to God.

Philippians 4:6

———

Pray constantly.

1 Thessalonians 5:17

Lord, remind me of the importance of prayer. There are so many times that this world distracts me from spending time with You. Father, I know that I should spend more time with You. Take away the distractions that keep me from You and allow me to grow deeper with You. Amen

Understanding the sovereignty of God is something that will naturally flow from a person's faith. When you have faith in God and all that He is, praising Him is something that just seems right. We serve a God that created the universe, that brought us from dirt, that freed slaves, that rained fire, that parted seas, that gave us His Son, that had Him die for our sins, that defeated death, that rose again, and will one day return. When we know this about God Almighty, faith comes.

The Lord does whatever he pleases
in heaven and on earth,
in the seas and all the depths.
    Psalm 135:6

———

A person's heart plans his way,
but the Lord determines his steps.
    Proverbs 16:9

———

A king's heart is like channeled water in the Lord's
hand:
He directs it wherever he chooses.
    Proverbs 21:1

What should we say then? Is there injustice with God? Absolutely not! For he tells Moses, I will show mercy to whom I will show mercy, and I will have compassion on whom I will have compassion. So then, it does not depend on human will or effort but on God who shows mercy. For the Scripture tells Pharaoh, I raised you up for this reason so that I may display my power in you and that my name may be proclaimed in the whole earth. So then, he has mercy on whom he wants to have mercy and he hardens whom he wants to harden.

    Romans 9:14–18

We know that all things work together for the good of those who love God, who are called according to his purpose.

    Romans 8:28

Heavenly Father, teach me all that You are. Reveal to me daily Your sovereignty. There are so many different things that are under Your dominion. Remind me of those things each day. Allow me to see You when I see the wonders of this world. Allow me to recognize the things that are subject to Your hand. Amen

Being thankful is something that can almost be forgotten in faith. We have faith water will come from the faucet . . . so we lose thankfulness for the water that comes from it. We have faith that the lights will turn on when switched on, so electricity is not something you readily see people thankful for. God is no different; there are so many things that He does that we don't even recognize with a thankful heart. We have breath in our lungs, the ability to wake, and the ability to even read this sentence! How do we so easily forget to be thankful for these gifts.

Give thanks to the L<small>ORD</small>, for he is good;
his faithful love endures forever.
    Psalm 118:1

———

Rejoice always, pray constantly, give thanks in
everything; for this is God's will for you in Christ
Jesus.
    1 Thessalonians 5:16–18

———

Every good and perfect gift is from above, coming
down from the Father of lights, who does not
change like shifting shadows.
    James 1:17

For we know that the one who raised the Lord
Jesus will also raise us with Jesus and present us
with you. Indeed, everything is for your benefit
so that, as grace extends through more and more
people, it may cause thanksgiving to increase to
the glory of God.

    2 Corinthians 4:14–16

———

Let the word of Christ dwell richly among you, in
all wisdom teaching and admonishing one another
through psalms, hymns, and spiritual songs,
singing to God with gratitude in your hearts.

    Colossians 3:16

Lord, thank You for everything that You do each day. I know that there are many times that I overlook the gifts that You so frequently give. Father, allow me to recognize all of the gifts that You give each day. Allow me to be more aware of the things that You do for me, and remind me to be thankful for them. Amen

One of the biggest correlations with those who are wise is that they also seem to have faith. The wise walk with a certain level of faith that most cannot begin to comprehend. They have taken their experiences, learned from them, and grown from them. The wise have realized that coming through those experiences was granted by God. This gives them faith to make it through the future obstacles. You'll normally notice that one of the differences between a wise man and a fool is how they handle hardship. One looks to grow from it, and accepts the hardship. The other crosses their arms and complains until it's over. The wise have faith that there is a point to the hardship.

Teach us to number our days carefully
so that we may develop wisdom in our hearts.
    Psalm 90:12

———

Do not be conformed to this age, but be transformed
by the renewing of your mind, so that you may
discern what is the good, pleasing, and perfect will
of God.
    Romans 12:2

Yet to those who are called, both Jews and Greeks, Christ is the power of God and the wisdom of God, because God's foolishness is wiser than human wisdom, and God's weakness is stronger than human strength.

    1 Corinthians 1:24–25

———

Now if any of you lacks wisdom, he should ask God—who gives to all generously and ungrudgingly—and it will be given to him.

    James 1:5

Heavenly Father, allow me to recognize that there is a point to all things that You have allowed in my path. Allow me to see these tough times to be moments in which I can grow. Father, allow me to seek the wisdom of those that You have put into my life. Instill in me a spirit that desires to learn, a spirit that desires to grow in wisdom and in You. Amen

VERSE INDEX